It Looks Like Rain

Written by Zoë Armstrong

Collins

It looks like rain!
Giant clouds are growing darker in the sky.

2

A little raindrop tumbles from the clouds and lands on the hill.

Plop!

The raindrop trickles down the hill.

It rolls past fields full of sheep and horses, and other animals too!

It rolls past houses, a school and a child riding her bike in the drizzle.

It trickles all the way down to the valley, and into the river.

Splosh!

The raindrop travels for miles in the river. It flows under bridges, into towns and past a group of children playing in puddles.

It pushes steadily on, past a shop, a tennis court and a very soggy football match.

Eventually, the raindrop reaches the sea. There are lots of raindrops there!

Splash!

The sky brightens and the sun begins to shine.

The sun heats the top of the sea, and some of the raindrops begin to evaporate.

The little raindrop is turning into a gas called vapour.

The vapour rises up into the sky.

It is colder up there, and the vapour turns into clouds. It turns back into tiny droplets of liquid.

The clouds grow bigger and darker, until ...

It looks like rain.

Plop, plop, plop!

The little raindrop has been on a trip from the sky to the sea and back again.

This is how rain travels around the earth every day.

It is a steady flow that is always happening.

Most rain ends up in rivers and the sea, but some rain seeps into the ground.

Plants absorb rain using their roots, and give off vapour from their leaves.

21

How does rain travel around the earth?

🐾 After reading 🐾

Letters and Sounds: Phase 5

Word count: 272

Focus phonemes: /ai/ a /ee/ ey, y, e /igh/ y /oo/ u /ch/ tch, t /c/ ch /j/ g, dge /l/ le /v/ ve /z/ se /s/ se

Common exception words: of, to, the, into, are, their

Curriculum links: Geography: Human and physical geography

National Curriculum learning objectives: Reading/word reading: apply phonic knowledge and skills as the route to decode words, read other words of more than one syllable that contain taught GPCs; Reading/comprehension: drawing on what they already know or on background information and vocabulary provided by the teacher

Developing fluency

- Your child may enjoy hearing you read the book.
- Take turns to read a page of text. Check your child notices the sentences that are exclamations, and use the correct intonation and tone of excitement or surprise. Point out the ellipsis (…) on page 15, and demonstrate how to pause to suggest the passing of time.

Phonic practice

- Point to **evaporate** on page 11. Challenge your child to separate the syllables as they sound out the word. (*e-vap-or-ate*)
- Repeat for the following words:

  page 9: e-vent-u-all-y

  page 12: va-pour

  page 19: stea-dy

Extending vocabulary

- Ask your child to choose the correct synonym (word with a similar meaning) for each of the following:

  soggy (*brown, wet*)   eventually (*finally, lately*)   drizzle (*fog, light rain*)

  trickles (*runs, dries*)   brightens (*shines, lightens*)
- Discuss their choice and the word meanings, checking in a dictionary if necessary.